Death & Friends

Jon Anderson

DEATH & FRIENDS

University of Pittsburgh Press

Acknowledgment is made to the following publications in which some of these poems first appeared: *Choice, Field, Hudson Review, Intro #1* (Bantam), *Iowa Review, New American Review, Northwest Review,* and *Tri-Quarterly.*

"The Parachutist" was originally published in *The New Yorker*; "Of Government," "The Mouths of the Poor," "The Next President," "Creative Writing," "The Robots, the City of Paradise," "Rowing at Dawn," and "It's the Beginning; So Much for Sentiment," in *Poetry.*

The epigraph is from *Death and Sensuality* by Georges Bataille. Copyright 1962 by Georges Bataille. Reprinted by permission of the publisher, Walker and Co., New York.

Grateful acknowledgment is made to Steve Orlen & David Schloss for their assistance and encouragement in the preparation of this manuscript.

ISBN 0-8229-3202-4 (cloth)
ISBN 0-8229-5217-3 (paper)
Library of Congress Catalog Card Number 70-117469

Manufactured in the United States of America

for Linda

Contents

III

We are attempting to communicate,
but no communication between us can
abolish our fundamental difference.
If you die, it is not my death. . . .

> Georges Bataille,
> *Death and Sensuality*

I

The Parachutist

Then the air was perfect. And his descent
to the white earth slowed.
                                    Falling
became an ability to rest—as

the released breath
believes in life. Further down it snowed,

a confusion of slow novas
which his shoes touched upon, which seemed
as he fell by

to be rising. From every
small college and rural town:
    the clearest, iced blossoms of thought,

but gentle.
                    Then the housetops
of friends, who
he thought had been speaking of his arrival,
withdrew, each from another.

He saw that his friends
lived in a solitude they had not ever said aloud.

Strangely he thought this good.

    The world, in fact,
which in these moments he came toward,

seemed casual.
Had he been thinking this all along?
    A life
where he belonged, having lived with himself

always, as a secret friend.

A few may have seen him then. In evidence:
the stopped dots
of children & dogs, sudden weave

    of a car—
acquaintances, circling up
into the adventure they imagined. They saw him drop

through the line breaks
and preciousness of art

down to the lake
which openly awaited him.
                Here the thin
  green ice allowed him in.

Some ran, and were late.
These would
forever imagine tragedy

(endless descent,
his face floating among the reeds,
unrecognized), as those

who imagine the silence of a guest
to be mysterious, or wrong.

The Trucker

Elevators, like great oaks
rise into the evening, and when they descend
you hardly know yourself.
                            All night
the fair, shadowed cab light
shone on the trucker's face. If only
he had learned to think like that!

Some extremes, but much benign lack of interest,
for which the heart gradually opens.
. . . patiently working, bringing cattle

from Denver, sorghum, oats,
butter, wheat and pigs from the Midwest,
steel bars, the body

with its different nightly smells . . .
He wanted to walk the length of Kansas.
The years had not even been difficult,

but like the stars
he watched from the speeding cab,
spaced unevenly . . .
so many particular events.

Pierrot Without Memory

Leaves, like the shadows
of flying birds, turn at the window, now
this way, now that;
    unsure of where in this he belongs,

he sees himself
at a great distance in his dream:
running, now standing, just as he does daily,

but in the image's hands
are flowers, representing nostalgia,
    poor blues and greys. Then his dream

takes the shape of guarded biography, wherein
the dreamer
removes his hands from the world's face,

letting the arms drop, the uselessness,
rather than be wrong.

So he is transformed into the moon, a light
within stone
    which only may bear witness.
At last he is himself,

bearing his head, a great
liquid globe, into the streets. Of those of us

who are not awake,
he alone does not beg to be relieved.
    His part in this is only radiance.

Give me your love, poor blues and greys.

The Wars of Adolescence

Think of the soul.
The soul thinks entirely of the body.
The body is out walking. The soul, in a silk jacket,
moans for its destructible friend.

The Civil Aeronautics Board leaped into the mountains;
they were seeking a cause.
A dress blew laconically toward them.
It was preceded by teary handkerchiefs, not unlike souls.

Later we compared notes, as at college.
The pilot and crew, having passed up these ridiculous flights,
were out walking.
Suddenly one looked up.

Trembling with anxiety, I looked up your address,
your dress.
Every spring another attempt was made.

What Keeps Us Grinning at Night

We thought sex was a root.
It would grow crooked, arthritic
& hard, very
relentless, serious, positive . . .

Those were the days! —
We could have inched into the earth;
we could have eaten for centuries
of the fat black;

we were gropers & long things.
Skinny & white,
we extended like tendrils
getting at the absolute.

Listen, as far back as you can remember
wasn't it quiet?
Wasn't it damp, you sluggard?
Wasn't the skull's wetness, whiteness

under your wife's face
what kept you grinning at night?

Creative Writing

The heart is a violent muscle; it opens & shuts.
The subject is death.
The subject is also laughter, the bravery
of girls, nine in a row.

In each face a hole opens.
Nine tiny stars of nervousness spin languidly out.

Sweethearts, death is blind,
he'll run up & down your bodies.
Death, with a dog's face
goes running through the Women's Dorm;
he has neither breasts nor jewelry.
Counselors run in his shadow, shouting Here,
We're all Christians here!

In the old country, everybody was Jewish.
Everybody had the smell of clothes soaked in a hot tub
and they learned to lament the fallen, the falling,
the about to be born.
Birth was painful, a long vibration
like the intake of breath after laughter.

I don't want to trouble you; you're entering history.
Your flesh is the moon's, gradual & broken.
Those boys are no consolation; they'll circle you,
    inscrutable calligraphy,
with no place to land.

I'm going to think about death until
my mouth runs. I'm going to look at death
with a face terrible as his own.

I don't want to scare you;
after death there are two alternatives,
both heartless:
memory & forgetfulness.

A Song for Children

Where are the tired adults
we must court & entertain?
We are helpless, like history,
we do not want to begin.

Now to be bathed, now to be kissed,
now to be put to sleep.
We are soft dolls, or cups,
the silences they keep.

To Kill a Man

He who has not killed a man
Moves through the air in a daze.
Amharic warriors' song

Perhaps in snow.
Certainly by hand.
His, in your own,
grows slack.

Now it is permissible
to sit quietly.
His fingers tighten
in yours. Hours

watching the sun
move, the snow waver.
Then it's dark.
The field freezes.

Come out, rabbit,
this is safe—
And the mice, small
spots of nervousness.

But trust me,
there is nothing
left to lose
or witness.

The white owl
passes overhead.
The fox sleeps.
How can you know

his dream? I can.
Here is the hand.

The Desire of the Blind

In confinement I dignify myself,

having at the one end
    of my intention
wilderness: pain so cold or sunless,
into which I would set you free.

You who are blameless, therefore not enriched;
who have two good legs, or one,
    an eye that goes outward,
come forward.
                    This is my eye,
which you may enter.
Here, first, are nerves burned back, blackened;
& continual twilight
like waking at an early hour.

    Deeper,
that landscape which, although whole,
has not been touched by light.
    Here there is no direction: nerves so sensitive

they are offended by you.
Against fear, open your hand:
    the eye of the palm
is faint, but means communion.

Starved, weightless in despair,
may you at last break forth into a clarity,
    the silence of which is terrible.

Therefore without solace

and at land's end
whisper me secrets which are small
   and shameful.
Out of my own materials (envy

& the saint's choiceless vocation) I can build
for us a house
which for love of the dark will endure.

Salt

The salt is snowfall
over the white bandage of our sleep
through one night,
& in the morning there is dust
like frost. In fact, first winter: abstinence.

So we awaken, & thinking of: *snow*,
we set out blocks. All the dark faces,
shadowed as the past,
those we had been meaning to preserve,
lean, like cattle,
above the salt & eat.

                       Again
that salt, which is like snow, falls
steadily between us & the daylight.
Now the ancient metallic aftertaste.

Now the landscape, blurred,
though still protective; the wives & sons
who wave from windows, then
retreat, comfortably, into shadowed rooms.

We think of: *family*, a country
we envisioned, but could not create;
& of love, which like the snow
fell endlessly, though we could not remember

to speak well enough of it.
We think only of the eternal.
Utah, a white sea, shines for us.
Someone is walking
over that ocean of snow, hands outstretched.

He will just touch these dark lids, closing.
He will just enter these bodies of salt
in which he meditates.

13

The Eye of the Traveler

i

Grey genitals of coffee
hang over the cup's lip. Even the egg
is bland in its spoon, a mild offense,
though warm. In the morning news
the wars go on. Before this meal
you want to believe that an affirmative
angel will lean down. For grace,
you say for grace.

ii

Some men advance with aprons.
One drives in a truck, dropping sawdust
in a narrowing circle to be spread.
Now the animals enter; though they
are foolish and not to be told,
we believe they die in pain.
In January they slept standing,
a line of cold foreheads, facing north.
Now one will breathe like an opened faucet
down to the soft, hot floor. Whether
in dignity or confusion, he bows.
His snout cracks like a stone.

iii

When you were driving to Tucson, your eye
went by itself, without destination,
for it was remarkably cast down.
That hitchhiker, who should
have been curious, or a gracious mirror
to shine back on you, slept
sitting up. Was he formidable?
You thought he carried the cold
iron of experience in his boot,
but he kept it there. His tongue clucked
lightly in his sleeping cheek.

iv

Maybe the angel is experience. The animal
and the traveler might know him by belief.
We move into the next storm
and the slaughterhouse without regret.
It is morning; the animals fall down,
their bodies silently steam.
Coffee scalds the air above the cup.
Maybe like a miracle because it
is common, a man who walks upright
drinks his coffee and departs.
His head nods as he walks, a blind,
or holy, affirmative machine.

II

The Campaign for Peace in Our Time

Once in an adolescent sweat
we planned all night to be righteous;
to be never without poverty
and always unreasonably gentle
(how could they forgive us?)
like fathers, to our wives.

The campaign for peace in our time
distracts, like the coffee talk of saints.
Compassion is a kind of whip
I don't use well—but if I were ardent,
walking into the fields
or over the snow with a step less social,
then I could walk forever . . .

The saint flagellates himself; it seems
to be another man. Not pain,
but the aesthetic of pain is learned.
He knows there is no reward for being hurt.
Slowly he strips his skin.

What a beautiful mistake!
You, or I, the poor men—we who are
neither gentle nor killers in a bad cause—
did we find that vacant, flayed skin
and mistake it for a coat?
We are terrified, we are pleased
to wear it, into the streets
and at last to our journals and beds.

From that coat of pain
a certain voice which is half ours
speaks openly, and entertains our lives.
But the campaign for living with ourselves
which was a saint who became free
is moving swiftly now into the fields,
gliding over the snow—
a heart of great lightness, grown
altogether practical and strange.

The Solitude of High Office

John Kennedy

Imagine it: a man whose fingers
grow like redwoods into the century,
a row of proclamations.
It is a partial change: into the lives
of men who are themselves
lives of their fathers, the stories
told to them as children.

I mean the stories of how kings wept,
in the arms of their children,
and the solitude of high office.
We saw the streets we had been walking,
not of gold, but stone.

By his death, of a value
not intentional, saying in the slow traffic—
and when there is silence
like a tree spread over the picnic
or standing in the child's room—
here again is the story of kings: now
how we must love ourselves.

The Next President

From the cracked bodies of insects
for his protection
we will construct a shell of brown enamel,
which at the first blow will shatter.
We make ourselves ready by treachery.

For his fingers, eight keys,
which in continually changing combination
will allow him entrance, into his house & office.
These are named force, childhood, accuracy,
the cave, potty, Sebastian Bach,
the key & need. At his prayer
the crossing of thumbs will signify assassination.

The grave:
topped by carved angels, in the manner of New England,
each with a child's face.
Here in each pupil we have bleached the stone
where the bullet may enter.

But he will be the one we do not murder,
who has no place in our affections.
He leaves an alternative:
we may punish
ourselves without cause, & be free.

He will have so little need of us
as to rise daily from the dark Potomac
into our contemporariness, like mercury in bread,
the eight keys raised to bless,
the eyes blind, fixed within.

The Robots, the City of Paradise

Out of the knowledge you mysteriously left
came oil, steel, art,
ways to duplicate ourselves.

Year-of-Our-Makers-X, world without nations,
wherein we walk, fearless, under the dead lamps,
hardly bothering to care. Our shadows
cross your dark shop displays; our purposes
slowly forgettable, though faithful to your plan.

Your aluminum police, our angels, soar . . .
Everywhere the new pattern
is ourselves, believing in necessity, as you
in our memories did not.

City of Paradise: commitment to a powerful,
abandoning instruction. We stand
like citizens, like lambs without banners,
under the best of all lives,
liking it, yours.

The Spoons

We're eating your lies,
ashes in silver spoons;

impossible not to hate you!
No, not your lies—

your demands,
burned, your plans for our lives.

We should be done.
The spoons are still cracking,

are we beating our skulls?
Like children, like

convicts. Thank you,
at last we are doing everything wrong!

The Mouths of the Poor

The mouths of the poor are grinning, lasciviously,
from windows as you drive by.
They are making plans, in doorways, in alleys,
under that light that sways on a long rope.
Here are some plans: bread, sex, meat . . .
Here is a new vocabulary, you aren't included,
for how do you kill a policeman, how do you kill
a *poor* policeman, how do you know, you don't.

The mouths of the poor followed you home, into
the unlit garage. Who closed the door?
You found one, stuck, like a kiss, to your fender.
The mouths of the poor are a fetish, let them
eat feet. How do you kill a thing like that?

In your garage you beat that thing
with a broom, does it bite? One is not dangerous;
here is the noise it makes, squeak.
If you beat it with a broom, it will run;
if you push the wrong end of a broom
between those fat lips, will it choke?
Will it make its report? It's hidden behind
the trash, under an oily rag.
Is it stuck to your foot?

The mouths of the poor are moving, laboriously,
upstairs; are you asleep? Your bedroom door
is covered with kisses; are you awake?

The teeth of the poor are not bone.
They are splintering, like anthracite.
They are melting down, like hot cheese
over those gums. Can a thing like that hurt?

Like a martyr's wounds, let them eat vinegar,
let them eat salt until they cannot whistle for help.
Who asked for this, moving along your flesh?
The mouths of the poor, exactly like
the mouths of the rich, are hungry, pulling
through the intestines in your warmed bed.
Can they see their mistake?

Like the man who ate children, inducing,
at last, that love which had eluded him,
those mouths want too much of our lives.
One desires the paint from your station wagon.
Here is another, eating television:
the disappearing comedian's mouth wades, into
that silence which he nervously examines.

How can we tell them? What can we feed ourselves?
My mouth, on my wife's, really desires speech.
The man who ate children, in his cell
discovered that little things, nails and dust,
produced the same result—but much too late.
You want to say something small,
it would save your life. The bodies
of the poor, like bags of damage,
are waiting for your report.

Of Government

Of necessity, the women lie down like maps.
The men are beautiful divisible numbers.
Tragic & insubstantial, *he* moves on *her* landscape,
a particular sequence we will call believable.

So now we are adult. Each of us
is a little mother, rediscovering seriousness:
how around a table the arrangement of dolls
frowned, without breasts, into their tea
one day and refused to speak.

In bed, we are as political as children.
It reaches *that* far, the idea of government,
controlled movement of traffic & arms.
Then we are masses of emotion
needing direction to be trusted?

The marriage directive is: Adjust.
The movement of men over women is friendly,
and, for a moment, light, then stalls.
Then slides away, like a land mass
into the sea.
                         The directive of government
is: Diplomacy. Like courtship,
it fears and displays the erotic;
like marriage, it cultivates the bored.

Boredom, the single indignity worth repetition.

Some indifferences take care of us,
but eventually each is an angry father:
the artist's scorn for his audience;
hatred of the child for the parent
who, by love, permits no escape.

Failing at love, we find it was not important.
Better to be honest than to be human,
though both are contained in a pure, relentless anger:
hatred of opposites, of sex, of directives,
hatred of ourselves, and boredom with that hate.

So we move toward heaven, man and wife
and nation, not hoping to find it,
but by some violences done to ourselves
(by marriage, by government) to reveal ourselves.

Lacking belief, we are the dolls we once kept.
One day they would not be arranged
but stared into *our* government (which was,
we then believed, of love), were undeceived,
and trusted, at last, the richness of the world.

It's the Beginning; So Much for Sentiment

But when we trudged uphill, noting
the sooty mass of snow, watching the chimneys
grow dark with twilight; there we were,
and the way was tedious. Time to procrastinate.

Here is a heap of fat: it sucks
its cigar, makes plans; it even contemplates.
Your neurosis, an unbelievable pressure,
can stand in itself like a cow.

In the face of the loved friend
you see a door, his own loneliness;
beyond, the meadow and trees.
The secular root of the bad dream
was always ourselves, most difficult.

So there we were, and it *was* the beginning,
chewing our useless intentions.
Out of them came soft, metallic gowns.
It was a kind of progress: we slept,
dreamless, cold and protected.

Oh but daily we were all hot with lamentations!
Slowly they grew into the wrong mountain:
a strategy, destroy it!

Depend on the friend's face, his good intent,
his willingness to allow some deception.
An unbelievable pressure is lean and hungry.
Starve it, love it, put your head into it,
it is the new year, build into it
instruments of instruction which will terminate.
Is it the right beginning? We march into it;
it is open all around like a meadow;
we come naked, sweet as tea, secular, joyless, intent.

28

"All We Are Saying . . ."

All they are saying will turn you
against yourself, reversing
    the flow of commodities

& occupations, into instruments
of self-analysis; all they are saying
    will leave you naked

among enemies: consciousness of age;
the inconstancy of meaningful experience
    into which you must nevertheless

entrust everything, & in all
hopelessness take up this grief
    they cannot bear alone.

Afraid to be alone; afraid not
to be alone. My brother's eyes fill
    with a terrible regret:

his inevitable death, &
the impact of love, from which
    I, too, desire protection.

Amid the vulnerability of these
young, who love each other,
    we must be shy &

look down. All they are saying
will hurt you forever, as it
    will hurt them,

as it has hurt us who desired justice
but forgave ourselves too easily
    & too much.

This is your brother, his truth
will be a weapon against you,
    he is so much

like you. All he is saying
is redemptive, will give you back
    the exactitude of pain.

III

Believer in Pain

Jerusalem
the city a word
the word is *illuminant*

or *oil* a lubricant
I desire to be magnanimous
it is desire

a man's joy
a woman's pain upon
which all the nations rise

in the dark
at the olive's center
we lie disturbed

in death the flesh oil & solid
in love squeezing it forth
in birth skidding out on it

wounds blackened
of the saints
oiled & bound in Jerusalem

oil of the wringing of hands
castile of the boiled animal
the greases of labor

Jerusalem hidden
in a field of petroleum
well hidden inside the sentry's whistle

in the graves
flesh waits for the rain
the sewers glisten

the soul
in its oiled boat
believer in pain come forth

A Letter

for David Schloss

i

I put my soul in a tin dish.
All night
the possum lapped.

Next I put

I put my brain in the tin dish,
it was slick.

I put my brain in the tin dish,
god-awful.

I put my brain in the tin dish,
the brain pan,
the bowl. I didn't want it.

ii

One night
my hand became a tarantula.

But I kissed its head,
I put my mouth down in the dark fur, turned
it over, breathed

into the warm belly of palm.
And such repose, David,
came over me . . .

But the other one,
the hairless one,
was a hand. It shook in fear.

Now I have two hands, no
intellect, and each
refuses to cut off the hated other.

33

iii

Every year I feel older; it's normal,
a task I don't love, & haven't
the time to hate.
Powerless, now

I walk out.
And, inarticulate, I breathe into the faces

of the undergraduates. A girl
said, "Mr. Anderson,
you *know* so much," & I touched her; but

my good hand
ran along my face: its wilderness.

iv

And, David,
but for love of you (& some
others) I'd give up. You said,

"I can't find my life, either."
It falls all winter;
it falls into your hair & your eyes, making

them wet again:
the lost freshness
for which we hurt ourselves, and write these letters.

Spring Song

The raccoon lay down at dawn,
its little feet were pointing upward.
Even the tourists are sick.

And the daily, beneficial light
which had traveled a long time
toward us, lies on its head
in meadows, and against trees.

It begins to surround us,
lighting the leaves easily,
some bark, the earth, a green stone.
We spread sheets over the ground.
Love is good. Who are you?
If I'm sullen, you'll mother it.

Just under the blue scum
of a pond, we, facing up, see
ourselves dramatically touch.
I'm sick of it all, I pull
your little breasts.
                          Oh it is
another morning; starving,
I've come around. Love,
muddy bitch, nothing is right;
it is the year of regrets,
why does the light come down?

Lecture with Slides

The city, very white, extends
for a few miles; around it
is nothing important. Its streets
are not crowded, or dirty.
Partially submerged in entrances,
the women are indistinct; dress, often
the color of dust. Happiness is not
important. If you have been walking, it seems
endlessly, in those blazing streets
there is always a shop open.

A traveler from the Mediterranean spoke.
But it was just beyond remembering;
nor did he interest you.
The problem might be selfishness.
But if so, it is intentional, like
a man turning from love. Later you made
some remarks, meant to be polite,
which he took seriously.

And in the classical grey women
there was that lovelessness
you sought. You were approaching
a middle age. Had you
anything to say for yourself?

Rowing at Dawn

The summer of 1940
has risen again, slowly, like the white
incandescent back of a swimmer.
Here are the unborn: one light
in a lightless pond
into which the first signal
will be courage, causing them pain.
Into their dream
the oar of the new world dips & pulls.
Slowly the rain
is light upon their shoulders, *Come,*
here is July, the month
of your birth, into which water runs.
All over Europe
sirens unwind into the morning.
The parents moan, like nations bearing sheep.

It is possible to believe in the day
without confusion, to find
the light coming between some trees,
unmemorized. It is possible to move
openly among one's discontents,
to love the enemy, to bear
witness with an honesty which is kind,
because direct. Sleeping
I believe this. But in a dream
the voices of the unborn clarify and rise:
    Come, it is still the beginning
    we will eat the dark
    muscle of our mothers' hearts
    and drift forever into evening . . .

Drowning

Out of my hands. Awhile
without breath, letting go, some stories
in which I recognize myself—
that solemnity
which in a former life I kept from you,
that, here, is sleep.
So let me go.
Resigned, I am at last kept wholly
only by you.
Drifting above your bed,
here are my hands,
head, feet, the five white islands
turning & joined.
                  Only when you sleep
without memory,
my body is like bread, coming apart.
Released, the blood rests
or falls, drawn downward into your lungs—
your breath is small,
dark clouds which dissipate.
Slowly, almost without weight
the tubes & secret chambers
of my body fall toward you, covering,
then dissolve. What love
you had for me
rests, a cleared intelligence on your face.
Now it is nothing human: water,
or air,
or charity without belief.

Walking Barefoot

In the morning,
I'm not used to it . . .
and the dew
burns; I had thought
to give up every kind of pain.

There is the other life
without passion or memory.
It goes alongside.

It is the turtle's shadow.
It is the snail's shadow.

In each of my steps the grass darkens,
filled with discontent.

Thinking of Death

The sleep was in me.
He was thinking
of that night on the beach, the sleeping bag
a coat full of weariness.
Just below his head
the water, a dark animal
with no face,
advanced. He dreamed of combing his hair.

Some men marry, he said,
but I am thinking
of death, always. What a gentle wife.

In November, 1968,
I'm sick on pills and sleeplessness;
my gentle wife is no help
though she touches my hair.

Who can we pray to next, who has
a bag of salt
in which to carry us home?
I have never been so far from my own death,
so far from the personal.

Walking in the Open

i

Walking in the open
with three friends, we came
slowly out of our conversation
up a small hill, then down, breathing,
to this place I now set before myself again:
a field, where I felt recognized.
There was no tree, but myself
at the center of three friends,
each of us vulnerable,
each of us silent and walking . . .

ii

In the north I have come to imagine
the lakes are cold, filled
with clarity. And in their houses
I believe my friends, who
are alone, shower and sleep.
Rooms fill with their breathing,
which will die. The fields
we have walked toward
are diminished; yards break outward
past landfall and the last,
desperate intuition: if I saw
you there, I would refuse you . . .

iii

But I want to be what you ask.
In that northern country
blood burns a trail; the snow
is hurt by it. I want to be hurt by it,
running with the small animal's terror
into the next thing, courage;
and, surviving, the necessity of care . . .

Beginning Again

I'll go there.

I can see myself close to the dead,
like a child with no coat,

like a man without words.
Then I will respect happiness.

My Parents

Their shoes don't fit.
Now they are walking into the forest.

Nothing is small enough for them,
they are so vulnerable.

Let the trees be *their* parents.
And to the little
dried-apple doll's face of my unconscious:

Keep them.
They are the honest.

The Photograph of Myself

Surely in my eyes that light is now lost,
or has deepened; and my hand, which
in the photograph seems tense
and strong, is less sure.
                              Is it
the right hand? Yes, it is still
lean, and larger now;

enough to hold this small, boy's hand
within it, like a son's,

perhaps to reassure him, as I do not
my own sons, who are not yet born.
   Across the grey garden

stand some men; I do not know them.

Nor, I think, does he. But they stand firm,
   a terrible simplicity
which will disappear. So, too, the other,
unknown, as far from him

as my living self, who again
clicks the shutter.
      He did not know it would reach this far.

   But it's not real, the boy,
myself, looking out at me but not seeing,

and the garden, which never grows.
      Good friend, believe me,
here I am, perhaps your best intention;

my hand can hold now your entirely small body.
   I can love you;
you are the friend's son, myself,

to whom I speak and listen.

Each Day Does That

It seems, before sleep, something has been dishonest;
I'd like it to have been the day.

It is the recognition of a circle, some mild agreement
made as a child to behave, by which I could assign
myself the center of all things: a passive nature.

I sometimes write from an "occupation"—mailman—cardiac—
those whose lives are honest because without perspective.
They begin to value their loneliness. They grow tragic
and beautifully antique.

If these could meet, say in a conspiracy designed to fail,
they might agree: "I never met a man I didn't like."
Of all confessions, the worst!

Had I arrived, I'd say: "Resignation, the acceptance of
the reasonably tragic, is why I made you." They would
tear up their former maxims and begin to compete.

Once I wanted my readers to cry; now it's my personnae.
Things are getting hot.

But the truth is I'm getting older. Most of my definitions
turn out to have been early promises, now more and more
forgettable.

Just before sleep, when I'm afraid, a few of those poems
which I had thought to be distant turn their small,
interested faces.

Never plain enough, or true enough, but their intention
turns my body, which had been weak with stubbornness,
toward home.

My parents lie like children in the dark. I'm not close
enough to hear them speak. But their love for each other,
which once seemed small to me, is there, and I can sleep.

The Honest Craftsman

Rain oils the backyard,
the leaves darken. How are the dead doing?
Do their lives lie with them?

One of my own, without invitation,
eases from my head
and circles the lamp.

*

A life did not care
for the slow, sensual rot of a neighbor: myself.

From this window I can see him
touch a leaf thoughtfully, and move on.
Good luck, you bastard.

*

I recall the journal of my grandfather,
John Ladd:
    "Rained, & cleared,
    48 degrees, March 18,
    1935, 2 p.m."
Five hundred pages of weather.

*

The old life
drops me a line: ". . . Suspect we are all
                        secretly without ambition."

Miles away
the dead are not even awake.

Summer Nights

Because of death, they are valuable.
A man waters his lawn.

PITT POETRY SERIES

COLOPHON

This book is set in Baskerville types. The Linotype cutting used here is the most faithful to the original eighteenth-century version, and was produced from a complete font cast from the original matrices found at Paris in 1929.

    The printing is directly from the type by Heritage Printers, Inc., on Warren's Old Style antique wove paper.

    The book was designed by Gary Gore.